SOFT SPOT OR SEDUCTION

THE LOVE OF ICHOR

SUMEET KUMAR

Sumeet Kumar

Sumeet Kumar , A adult who experiences many phases of love in his life , get broked many times , stands up every time and keep moving to the next phases of the life.In reality he is a writter as well as singer (as a hobby) . Very exciting and interesting fact about him is that he is author of New era i.e. he starts his journey of writing at the age when he was going to schools to get the study . His some famous works i.e. Maturity Of Love (Genre - Love),Privacy For Dream (Genre - Middle Class), Army Squad ofLove (Genre- The Seperation of Army Love), 5 Days of Love(Genre- Temporarily Love), Th e Endearment Of Love(Genre - Historical Era Of Love), Social Destruction Indo-Pak (Genre - The Story of The Love At The Time Of Division Of India And Pakistan), Middle Class Soul (Genre - The Dreams of Middle Class), The Accursed Kanatpur (Genre -The Horrific Story Of A Village), Wrong Number (Genre -The Suspenseful Physco Killer Story), The Secrecy OfDeadly Midnight (Genre - The Suspense About a Crime),Fragile Religious Of Death (Genre- The Death Of A TrustfulPerson), Nature Vs Science (Genre - The Future Battle Between Nature And Science In A Horrific Way), Generic Man (Genre - The Dream of I.I.T), The Unconsious 12 Hours(Genre - The Illusion At Stage Of Comma), The StrangeBurden (Genre - The Burden Of Love) , Her Existence (Genre- The Female Pain In The Society) , Jockstrap Prize (Genre -The True Story Of A National Athlete) , H Man [Hindi] (Genre - Superhero Tragic Story), H Man [English] (Genre - Superhero Tragic Story) , Maturity Of Love [Englsih] (Genre - Love) and many more are available on various geners on the offcial platform of **Amazon, Flipkart and Notionpress**. You can buy them from there.

Contents

Acknowledgements

Aman Kumar

Special Thanks to **Aman Kumar** who worked so hard in the preparation of this book. He has continually put with my passive voice, omission of words, and late night calls. You have been wonderful. Thanks to him for his precious time in reviewing proposals , individual chapters and early drafts, along with his suggestions on the applicability of the material to the world.

I
Warmth Love

There are some dreams in life which are never fulfilled and only their memories are sometimes different from us, because the dreams of those who are already unfulfilled, their dreams can come in our part and become completely cashless, have learned only one thing since childhood. If you will try, you will get the floor, no one has ever raised the veil from the mystery that after all, who is taking the name of the right effort, after whom we have to run, every day as soon as we cross the limit of effort, what will happen to the child now? What people? Never thought in life that so many accidents would come together in my deserted right world and if someone had to come to our gathering, then at that time we had said the happiness of our gathering, meaning in English, they were there. Of happiness, every witness in the world has a heart, this is what everyone believes, one thing that is even more surprising comes to the fore that this heart is not an ordinary heart, which is the only reason for your living, this heart is nowadays a Has become a sympathizer, that too for those people who have forgotten in the blindness of love that we cannot give the same heart to everyone. affection maybe only applies when a hero tells his heroine that I can't live without you my companions who can't walk without you and my heart is lost in the search of darkness and can't live without you What does it mean to say? And where do these people come and if there is no logic in their life, then we can survive it even if the feet are not in love, then life seems deserted, well let me tell you that this is my thinking. It is not at all necessary that love is necessary in life because if love is so necessary in life, then this world does not have money, feet, sleep, babu's thinking, moving feet, such a thing that they do not have love, nowadays because where there is love, humanity is also in general. Feet are seen, not everyone is capable of it, nor does it come in everyone's luck nowadays, that too by becoming a fortune, this world was as famous as it was today, it has become as much gimmicky, that too only because of one word which we are in love with. It is said that this is not a small health thing found in the market, by weighing it and applying the right price, we can give it to someone. Let me give it to you, it is a beautiful waste, which everyone likes in the beginning, after the passage of time, its enmity destroys us more and during the time we only think that I wish I would not forget the relationship for the witness. Life would have been different, maybe my dreams would have been different and my reality would have been different like: Every day's morning is not the same, like everyone's love is also not the same, there are many changes in life, then we get this fate. It is said that no one lives alone in the world because everyone has this cruelty, foot humanity, people have a lot of work, in the world everyone's thinking is wrong. Those people believe in their feet, even if they are not their feet, they give a feeling of belonging all the time and this is the people that we love, and when the time comes, we can do anything for them. If we do not have love, it becomes our last passion, so that neither we can ever separate ourselves from ourselves nor can we ever forget it. people would have easily said that go ahead, forget the joy in life and celebrate a new world of your own, foot why no one ever says that you are fine, what have you lost by going to his gathering, the silence which has been buried inside you. You can never separate yourself from standing, I have heard that in the world, we do VPR of people bodies To live with the feet, only for some time, the love does not see any reason, nor does he look at any evidence to say that he is a gentleman, this crook brings only one waste for everyone, the feet get better with time, so some love They are broken that only silence is visible in their gathering, people's love changes, it was also like a happy foot love, whose truth is two-sided for us, whose love is neither clearly visible nor dimly The memories of our souls always give us trouble, say no matter how good it is in the past We say to run many times, where neither his silence is heard nor his happiness is also a big reason behind it, and the child can understand the witness who has sacrificed himself many times for someone else and that reason The debate is so right that all the moments we have spent with a stranger say that they are happy, we have given our full determination to maintain a relationship, yet in the bowels we do not know to save the relationship and in life there is a relationship. Like regret it burns in our hearts and minds. One of the witnesses has said that people in love can do anything to stay together, they don't need any reason to stay with you, to share with you, to stay close to you For if the love is true and the condition is bad, then she will still be with you and she will never be able to take time off from you and probably I have made it true to a great extent and this is a fact, even if you feel it, then you will definitely get the love of feeling. I have only one problem that we give so much importance to the male witness which he is not capable of, I mean to say any relationship. What is the need to save on one side when the witness has given him this toad on the other side, we give many relationships tod to save him a relationship and in time, when we realize the feet, then our world is only dark at the time I don't have time to think, why should I say Who is my god, What will I be able to live without her Will my conspiracies be called Give me just one reason why You will not be able to forget him When you have called yourself and have forgotten those relationships, then why can't you forget him It is a matter of fact that we cannot forget him because to come to a witness, we have lost our souls. We have given up living to get a witness, this is not just my words, this girl is not doing only her bati in time, I am doing the conversation of the human society, which has told the pride of men that boys never rot. No, sir, have cried many times, even after bereavement themselves, they gave happiness to others. From the happiness of childhood to growing up, he has remembered the sorrow of a father, he has taken care of the dreams of his brothers and sisters. Key find: It is not of hearts. I can not write anything else in the part, yet there are some things in my mind, which I ask to be done in front of everyone, I tell them to free them from their silence, whatever pain is right, I have complained about all of them today.

> *"I don't need you*
> *I can handle myself*
> *The Pain that you have gifted me*
> *I can contemplate myself*
> *And it's not necessary that you only remember*
> *me in your mind.*
> *With time, someone else can also come in your*
> *life but i can love myself*
> *"*

Not everyone is lucky in this world and not everyone even ponders it, it is inevitable in love because it starts with saying that people often say that you are my only dream and that too the world which I also tell myself that I have read every heart of the world, have seen every face, have seen every dream being broken, it is true that somewhere in the path of life, the destination must have been connected, I have lost the whole world. words can't break feet, there are some people to whom love is nothing special, my enough is an intention, I don't have the power to burn myself in front of them, to lose everything in the gathering and make a part of silence and grace the time. I consider every one of his words. If every education of the time is right, it is not necessary and accidents are the same all the time. Let's do feet, we are human now, said, without any reason, everywhere else is involved, today there was a desire for something else to write. Where we had never told to come and someone used to say that we still try, there is an beginning in my part which compels me all the time that even today I should be deprived of his abuses. There is no word of happiness, every person does not get the feet of the feet Like the one who sells his feet every day for his own benefit and not because of anyone's compulsion, whatever I am saying today, I am going to say this. This thought may not suit everyone.

"What's missing in me that she had left me
In a filled gathering , she made me a mirror
and broke me.
A small smile which comes from his mouth
every day with his abuses
Now that small smile had left me alone and broke
me."

II
Jump To Inferno World

It is said that the written fate can never be erased and someone's first love is also like this, if the dream is made in the spirit of ruin, then the writing of fate is also not special and every witness in the world is aware of the waste of money. The one who has saved his relationship with pure intensity, in fact, this life has also been found in a recommendation, which we all are aware of, not everyone is ready for it It is in your fate These few moments of love get a common letter from him who is infidelity, he probably stays close to us all the time, just like the anger, which is also necessary to live, after a few moments, his hurt also deserts us if love is played If you understand, then maybe his shadow can go ahead and become the reason for your death and this is not a tradition of a minor road, which is hot. I will ruin you only once and then will set you free, this will destroy you bricks every day every day that even the recommendation to live is shown the pond of death In love, it is often the ones who are used to that pain of pain. Who can never become your companion with you in that part, nor your love, the smile of a small child remains safe only till the scars of youth do not touch us, in this world only one tenant and one tenant To live in the world, there is a need to pay many prices and its owner is none other than the upper one whom we remember all the time in our sorrow and happiness, the world logs can forget its relationship, then the man is never the uppermost because every At the time, the shadow of the Supreme Lord is present with us, which we also know by the name of our gathering fear and the word of faith moves forward when something valuable comes in our part, if I say directly in words, then wealth and Love is exactly the same because after losing both of them life seems deserted every time like a flight of words The education of long pain progresses the same way, that's why I will not ask to move forward nor recommend it, so we leave the destination of wastage in this unfinished journey and I will wish you all in such a way. The floor says to walk with feet, where love was in the words of silence, which all of you can only feel, if you ever want to realize the dream in charity, then it is necessary for him to be a waste before starting his autobiography, there are some things that Share I say to do, even if there is love between two people in the world, it is necessary to recommend support for them to live together. When we come to feel it, then this need is visible in front of our eyes, that there has been love somewhere in the world, but that need is also long in their part because neither love is need without love nor love without need, these two are the same. One can never live without the other, nor can they ever be separated from each other, if two bodies go together in direct words. It is not necessary to be puberty in life in both the world's world, because it is necessary that these are the steps of our life which we call maturity.

"I have not applied for any kind of love, nor do I need any help.
But for the shake of the conincidence , the time which i have invested in remembering her.
These days I talk about happiness without any hesitation nor any help."

It is said that there is enmity in the world that destroys a witness, yet why do we request to live with it, I have walked barefoot on every floor, I have burnt someone's charity in his yards, I still ask questions about my gathering Why does it not end, I ask myself every day. My feet is because of someone else, in my short life, I have seen many big dreams and saw such dreams, which had no hope of fulfillment, yet I kept moving forward in their path, Well I meet my small world in my small world I am only my mother who has taken care of me since childhood, has fulfilled all my dreams, which I had forgotten long ago, although my mother never used my dad's surname because she would never bring me in her shadow Used to say and there is a big reason in the middle of it, which I want to bring in front of you all. happiness is such that mother used to be very rich family then and dad middle class family seh says that love is possible between two humans only when their status is , otherwise there are many work such relationships which can be called right sex, they are also final. Till the time dad and mom met in college, dad was also a scholar and mother was also in love between them, because the status of both of them used to meet a lot of times. She went ahead and made some friends and in the end both of them fell in love. In every relationship, there is a need to compromise, so how can she stay away from father and mother's relationship? Dad even though he was a scholar. A lower middle class family used to live together, so if grandfather had come to know about this, he would never have adopted their relationship, it was my mother's wish, it was not such a thing at all because when mom and dad ran away and got married, then grandpa They had searched a lot for both of them and to this point they even put their money sari in search of both of them. Time was against dad because dad had threatened dad that if he didn't stay away from his daughter, he would kill her life and his family and dad's family also had similar thinking of lower middle class family. Her specialty was that she would never bow down in front of anyone, except the one above, she had respect on one side and on the other hand, the rich mother also knew very well that her relatives would not be adopted by the society at all and perhaps her father would also be well. Whatever mom and dad thought was right for them at that time, they say that for the love of both of them, the relationship which was made with great love, breaks with time And this world's biggest tradition is to love, and on the other hand, what we only make a seal, when the time comes to remove our silence, when its need is over, then we leave it too. It has been said many times in the past that love is that VPR whose border is also the work of prostitute then, well when the mother and father ruined for getting married, then what is the matter at that time. She didn't know because mother had just said at the time of her friendship that she was going on a tour of their friendship and on the other hand dad told her family that she was going out for a job interview that too Bombay because Both of them knew that if suddenly he ran away for a complete, he could have been caught because my grandfather was just an ordinary person, he was a very big diamond vaccine, so every big witness took every small body from him and gave him and mother very good health. I used to think that till then he was engaged in his holdings in his city and Grandfather had worked hard to make his name and he used to say that my father should be like him first and then he should come and ask for mother's hand. If true cow then grandfather was not at all wrong at that time because people in the world tell love to weigh money with money, be it an arranged marriage, it is love kumarriage till then girls are given to our society, that too to spend the whole life with such a witness who She doesn't even know that well, I'm not saying at all that it is wrong to do an arranged marriage, feet should not be respected by everyone. That she is near such a witness that she can never fall in love with him, nor can she think about him. To say that those people are good, it was meant that they should never lack anything because from childhood, whatever the mother had asked for Grandfather, he never felt like it, it was not that she had sons, she had two sons. Were and my mother was too young to be all of them mother was very scared when dad gave her surgery and told her that your father has threatened me to die and my family too feet I don't care for me Kirti (Kirti Sharma who? My mother is only my family is worried about my feet, I can't live without you hard, nor can you stay away from you for a moment, so are you ready to say with me for life, then what was the mother's thought and nothing Dad was told yes to everyone, when Mia Biwi Aaj Toh Kya Karega kaji , his family friend told his mother that he should speak about Grandpa's tour. Because when he tried to run away, no one could catch him. Mother also came out of his house alone and the other dad also did the same, then both caught the train to Pune and when those two station feet met each other, he lefts friendship was already standing, that too the temple sun meant for them to get married, by the way, it was quite a film, I know that the thinking of the feet dad was very good because because of this, at the time, his sari had become very good and no one else Didn't even bother. It is when dad did not go to his house for a long time and mother also came to know about grandfather that mother has married that too with happy boy whom he did not consider worthy for his daughter that the feeling was a little weak at the time. It was because Grandfather had never thought that the daughter whom he has brought up with so much love and devotion, will become good because of his loneliness. And with time, people forget even their relationships, which are made with great dedication, so how long did Grandpa stay in his friends and when he would be able to take care of himself and stay apart from father and mother, so at this time he thought that He will adopt his daughter and son-in-law, I mean he will remarry both of them, that too in front of the eyes of the whole society, that's why he called them back in any way, says that behind every happiness there was a reason for sorrow. It is man's time some enmity had taken his place. Grandfather had adopted their relationship, my mother did not mother, I could never do the relationship, that's why he sent goons many times, that too to threaten the father's family. When Grandfather came to know about this, he threatened his mother, if you do something like this again, then we will destroy you not only from your house but also with your extravagance. I know neither respect nor respect if anyone is the most valuable in the world, then it is the wealth which is also in the gift of the pages. Even in the thoughts of a common man, I talked to Grandpa and my mother told him that now he will not do such a thing again. Mother was in Pune and father too then he himself had gone to take them back to the lane, when the father was not with him, asked the mother at the time that Akshat has said that at the time, the mother did not tell anything to the grandfather. Then she once asked mother, then mother said that Akshat has just gone out of work, he will come in a few days. Didn't ask anything out Said ok we live here for a few days then we all together will call our home We should walk, let's not miss the house anyway (Weeping mode Surely those eyes were clearly visible at the time and Grandpa had felt the silence of the mother, that's why he asked her many times what Akshat

said) What did he do with you He told fame He said He
didn't leave him if this is the case then I won't leave him
alive Said he said ? Dad is not in the world now! What what
to say What happened to you When did you happen
Mother when Grandpa was talking about her feet Later
when grandfather listened to him and when he saw tears
in the eyes of his beloved daughter then he was completely
broken inside. Akshat would have been with us today, my
father died, all this was never a mother I didn't tell me and
neither did Grandfather I didn't even come, I was still in
my mother's stomach when my father had died, after all
the accidents, Grandpa had brought mother to him, that
too in his city Delhi. Even though this story is incomplete,
feet I have to get something which is yet to be written
because my story has not even started yet, so how should I
end it? It is necessary for some time not to forget my past
and bad accident because I knew this thing that my past
has become an accident for my future and past.

"Nor there is any need of prayer
neither of any medicine
but the injury i got in the exchange of trust
the pain that my loved ones is purely extreme."

III

Razing Of Emotions

18 years later. **DELHI (TIHAR)**

By the way, I am in Delhi, I am very far away from the feet of the heart and that is because since childhood, till today, Grandfather has done me many times, today is my birthday, I am not happy in my feet at all because I have given my dad a lot today. I'm missing! I know wherever he is, I want to say something about him because he is watching me (Daddy Miss) There is one more thing that I want to share with you all that today is the first day of my college. Will be thinking that neither college nor college that too soon first then complete your school, he says that as Sakshi has no wealth in the world now, then he needs to study, my grandfather who gave me neither school's fodder Not allowed to disturb nor given a chance to see their studies, whatever you do, do it at home, they say that Surprisingly, another thing is that I have not gone anywhere in 18 years, nor did she go to Delhi. Look at the beautiful abuses, nor eat the chickpeas of Nathulal's feet on the roads and see the pride of our country, I mean the feet of India Gate is one thing, I have heard a lot about them and have heard so much that now I ask them to see them It also seems like a story, now I can't live in prison at all, it is in jail where relief is a little work from some jail, go matt here all the time On the other hand, when you think about murder, stay at home and you will get whatever you want, how can you say that I want freedom, that too many sarees, I have to roam in those abuses to eat Nathulal's parathas and go to Delhi. To feel the beauty, even though my childhood has passed in the four walls of silence and now I am not spending my youth, all these things I told my grandfather and mother, then I got the freedom to go out and I also got freedom in education Many meanings were applicable that two bodyguards will always be with you and you will not lose anything outside, nor will you do anything outside and take care of yourself and whatever you want, we will say then and will not do any mischief, I mean who is somewhere. And why don't I need so much security, I want to live a normal life in everyone's life, that too like others, I do not need everyone's care, even after saying all this, neither mother changed nor grandfather's words because of me Even after saying no, it is necessary to accept their words and take both of those bodyguards with you. Tons when it becomes a habit, freedom also deprives us of some time, well whatever it is, after so many years of happiness, I am going out somewhere, even if it is a college, foot now gives me a little I have got freedom and I will never let go of my hands, feet say that what we think will never happen in our life I started to get messy with me every time, looking at me, I don't know why my way was touching me They laughed seeing me and then turned to the side. For some time, I was feeling very uneasy because in the habit of childhood, one cannot see it in front of them in front of them. Were like: If you have seen a ghost, what was the foot like that, I am not an alien soul, everyone was surprised to see me, after some time it was realized that he Because of me, they were not scared because they were scared at this time because two bodyguards were also with me, they were also of the size of the cake and they both had guns, so all the students of them were scared seeing me. By the way, I visited my college so what the name only told, what did I do? it was feeling so much during the day that I did not know anything about when I went to college and when I have come in I forgot to tell the name of my college which is my grandfather It was Trinity High College, during the time when I took my eyes in heart then everyone knew who I am, it was happening in the whole class that I am very arrogant like others, I am arrogant who talks about anything. I was not doing many more and complete conversation, actually if I said the reality then it becomes my priority on that time ,thats why I didn't said anything but as I was not used to this atmosphere and above all my bodyguards who used to stay with me all the time to make me feel wayward For this reason, he does not allow anyone to come close to me, whenever someone tries to sit next to me, he lifts his shoulders and tells him. He would sit and at that time, even his professors were not telling him anything and even though the whole college belonged to my grandfather, then there is no place to speak, and if this accident would have happened at that time, then he would have to leave his job too. The party and the respect were also at the time when everyone was kissing each other, then the happy time is the entry of my queen, which neither the public nor the people were able to understand, yet I had lost my heart in the past, that too I have lost her beauty. It has been seen in the movies that when two strangers meet each other and as soon as they meet, when any one of them falls in love, then they call it as "love at first time " foot that was mine and a love was first college when he When I entered the class, all the others were looking at her and I am doing my thing to do my best. maybe , that I could go near and tell him that can you stay with me as long as there is life because the thing for life has become old nor feet say that often the thing which is beautiful is somewhere dangerous too And she was not a bit dangerous, it was too much I mean to say that she was a 2nd dan player and I also came to know when I was immersed in her dream and when she came close to me it meant to sit on my seat. When she came to sit on her seat, then my bodyguards again screwed her feet and beat her in the same story, even though she did not say my innocence, she had to obey her because the situation was out of control at the time. Seeing the gun which had gone out in front of the entire class at the same time, I was scared that even my feet were scared, what should I talk about my naturalness, that young time also did not move at all, he was my bodyguards. beat him even more and took China to his gun from him and my seat also means I had already sat on the side before fear in my own seat because I He had seen so many accidents for the first time in his incomplete life, then once the rain started happening to me, not about my queen, whose name was related to Vanni Malhotra, well now more accidents are bound to happen because when this thing happens Entire college knew, so grandfather did not know how: I can't keep dreaming About? Love is the only thing that can give life to a dead person and make the one who has life dead, I did not say at all that he should be different because what he did at the time of death was the only punishment. Was that he should be kicked out of college, nothing like that happened, I mean to say that what I thought did not happen at all and for the first time in my life, very happy about the accident, meaning my feet were not stopping my feet. I was not able to understand what to do, I was trying to kiss my grandfather at the bash because after that I can not tell the happiness that I got He also gave a long short to my bodyguards and I was still surprised in complete freedom foot that mother did not say anything once and why did this happen for the first time in 18 years, before that it was never even respected then why all of a sudden ?

"Moments have suddenly changed.
Did I am lost in a dreams.
And the sorrow that was in my part has now
turned into happiness

Did I am in the Angel's screams. "

At that time I was surprised and happy too because I got this happiness for the first time and I could never imagine it and I was happy because my voice was not going to hurt me now. I think about whether she also thinks about me No not at all Now that we meet now, I am in love and it is not necessary that she also has to be in love with me, to go to her feet, she will have to break the wicks or her feet. How to: If I tried to do things because of this she got angry with me, she attacked me too, then Grandfather came to know about this and after that he will take my freedom from China Can you help me with the above Even after all, I used to come to college every day in a necklace and see it everyday, my feet never dare to share with her, I don't know about shoes, almost 2 months have passed. Never talked to him, then finally my life took a turn and my world completely changed. I was a waste of my happiness, it was a waste of my past relationships and why am I saying this in the bottles, see for yourself

CONVERSATION

"

vanni : Oh mister! Why do you see me everyday?
me : But i don't know.vanni : Are you blind ?
me : i think yes , but in your love.
vanni : You will be beaten if you say this thing
again, understand it!
me : Ok beat me, but before that I want to say
something.

vanni : *what ?*
me : *...........*
vanni : *Now say what do you want to say?*
me : *i want to say that.......*
vanni : *What was there to say?*
me : *I love you when I stared at you for the first time, my heart and mind had lost my mind on you and when you saw that seat, I was really doing that to hug you, I did not say to beat you in the feet, that's why I Didn't do anything like this at the time you say thrash so thrash leg really can't stay apart from you now and if you still want to beat then walk outside in some corner and beat it because it is too many people i'm sorry and and love you! but please don't beat.*

vanni : *!!!!!!!!Saying all this I had closed my eyes because I knew that I am going to beat you for sure, that too in a lot of joints what I thought, I am not jealous again. What did he say to me.*
vanni : *oye ! Open your eyes now.*
me : *I am not going to open, do not beat me, if you have to beat then do not kill me here please!*
vanni : *If you open your eyes, I will not beat you, I have to say something.*
me : *Whatever you have to say, just say it but i will not open my eyes.*
vanni : *Stupid!!!!!! Be sure how I will hug you then, looking at your eyes, how will I respond to your love proposal.*
me : *Are u sure ? mmmm !*
vanni : *I love you too buggu, I thought you would say that because you were silent at the time*

*and there were so many college girls behind you, yet
you left them and loved me and never looked at
them and I liked you because of your love. Stupid I
love you infinite times.*
***me** : I had never thought that behind every
happiness there is a reason for sorrow, that too like
enmity, between our relationship, those incidents of
my past were connected, about which neither
mother nor grandfather ever told.* "

Well that past was none other than my dad oh mere dad not
Vaani,

dad means Now what is there to say on my part in I myself
have become a mystery when Vaani introduced me to my
dad Mother said that dad is no longer in the world, so what
is the face that I see every morning in front of me and the
bigger infidelity that my life has done to me is that what
voice is my sister If it is not, then it is my dad? Why are you
mixing it by saying that let's meet my dad in that way of
mirror which had broken legs and probably so broken that
neither is the recommendation to live anymore nor desires
and so many questions and answers not even a single what
was moment on that which was not complete, it is not a
dream, and if it is really a dream, then I say to die before
seeing it? And who was the right compulsion for the time
for which the mother hid all this from me, am I really her
son? Is he really my dad and if he is not, then he is doing
pictures in my and if this is also not true then who is my
dad ?there is no orphan in any place ? if I am an orphan? a
wastage orphan ? so why they love me ? Why ? love is and
if the voice of these saying comes to know then what will
happen .

"I have completed the journey
Now A few moments are left
And the recommendation of death is clearly
visible in front
Waiting is only for the grave which is going in
my own memories that are left."